King Victor and King Charles by Robert Browning

A TRAGEDY

From Bells and Pomegranates Number II

Robert Browning is one of the most significant Victorian Poets and, of course, English Poetry.

Much of his reputation is based upon his mastery of the dramatic monologue although his talents encompassed verse plays and even a well-regarded essay on Shelley during a long and prolific career.

He was born on May 7th, 1812 in Walmouth, London. Much of his education was home based and Browning was an eclectic and studious student, learning several languages and much else across a myriad of subjects, interests and passions.

Browning's early career began promisingly. The fragment from his intended long poem Pauline brought him to the attention of Dante Gabriel Rossetti, and was followed by Paracelsus, which was praised by both William Wordsworth and Charles Dickens. In 1840 the difficult Sordello, which was seen as willfully obscure, brought his career almost to a standstill.

Despite these artistic and professional difficulties his personal life was about to become immensely fulfilling. He began a relationship with, and then married, the older and better known Elizabeth Barrett. This new foundation served to energise his writings, his life and his career.

During their time in Italy they both wrote much of their best work. With her untimely death in 1861 he returned to London and thereafter began several further major projects.

The collection Dramatis Personae (1864) and the book-length epic poem The Ring and the Book (1868-69) were published and well received; his reputation as a venerated English poet now assured.

Robert Browning died in Venice on December 12th, 1889.

Index of Contents

ROBERT BROWNING – A SHORT BIOGRAPHY
ROBERT BROWNING – A CONCISE BIBLIOGRAPHY

NOTE

This was No. II. of Bells and Pomegranates and was issued in 1842, though it appears to have been written before the publication of Pippa Passes. The following is the advertisement prefixed to the tragedy when first published and always afterward retained.

"So far as I know, this tragedy is the first artistic consequence of what Voltaire termed 'a terrible event without consequences;' and although it professes to be historical, I have taken more pains to arrive at the history than most readers would thank me for particularizing: since acquainted, as I will hope them to be, with the chief circumstances of Victor's remarkable European career—nor quite ignorant of the sad and surprising facts I am about to reproduce (a tolerable account of which is to be found, for instance, in Abbe Roman's Récit, or even the fifth of Lord Orrery's Letters from Italy)—I cannot expect them to be versed, nor desirous of becoming so, in all the detail of the memoirs, correspondence, and relations of the time. From these only may be obtained a knowledge of the fiery and audacious temper, unscrupulous selfishness, profound dissimulation, and singular fertility in resources, of Victor—the extreme and painful sensibility, prolonged immaturity of powers, earnest good purpose and vacillating will of Charles—the noble and right woman's manliness of his wife—and the ill-considered rascality and subsequent better-advised rectitude of D'Ormea. When I say, therefore, that I cannot but believe my statement (combining as it does what appears correct in Voltaire and plausible in Condorcet) more true to person and thing than any it has hitherto been my fortune to meet with, no doubt my word will be taken, and my evidence spared as readily. R. B."

LONDON, 1842.

PERSONS
VICTOR AMADEUS, first King of Sardinia
CHARLES EMANUEL, his son, Prince of Piedmont
POLYXENA, wife of Charles
D'ORMEA, minister

FIRST YEAR, 1730.—KING VICTOR

PART I

SCENE:—The Council Chamber of Rivoli Palace, near Turin, communicating with a Hall at the back, an Apartment to the left, and another to the right of the stage.

TIME: 1730-31.

CHARLES, POLYXENA.

CHARLES
You think so? Well, I do not.

POLYXENA
My beloved,
All must clear up; we shall be happy yet:
This cannot last forever—oh, may change
To-day or any day!

CHARLES
—May change? Ah yes—
May change!

POLYXENA
Endure it, then.

CHARLES
No doubt a life
Like this drags on, now better and now worse.
My father may ... may take to loving me;
And he may take D'Ormea closer yet
To counsel him;—may even cast off her
—That bad Sebastian; but he also may
... Or no, Polyxena, my only friend,
He may not force you from me?

POLYXENA
Now, force me
From you!—me, close by you as if there gloomed
No Sebastians, no D'Ormeas on our path—
At Rivoli or Turin, still at hand,
Arch-counsellor, prime confidant ... force me!

CHARLES
Because I felt as sure, as I feel sure
We clasp hands now, of being happy once.
Young was I, quite neglected, nor concerned
By the world's business that engrossed so much
My father and my brother: if I peered
From out my privacy,—amid the crash
And blaze of nations, domineered those two.
'Twas war, peace—France our foe, now—England, friend—
In love with Spain—at feud with Austria! Well—
I wondered, laughed a moment's laugh for pride
In the chivalrous couple, then let drop

My curtain—"I am out of it," I said—
When ...

POLYXENA
You have told me, Charles.

CHARLES
Polyxena—
When suddenly,—a warm March day, just that!
Just so much sunshine as the cottage child
Basks in delighted, while the cottager
Takes off his bonnet, as he ceases work,
To catch the more of it—and it must fall
Heavily on my brother! Had you seen
Philip—the lion-featured! not like me!

POLYXENA
I know—

CHARLES
And Philip's mouth yet fast to mine,
His dead cheek on my cheek, his arm still round
My neck,—they bade me rise, "for I was heir
To the Duke," they said, "the right hand of the Duke:"
Till then he was my father, not the Duke.
So ... let me finish ... the whole intricate
World's-business their dead boy was born to, I
Must conquer,—ay, the brilliant thing he was
I of a sudden must be: my faults, my follies,
—All bitter truths were told me, all at once,
To end the sooner. What I simply styled
Their overlooking me, had been contempt:
How should the Duke employ himself, forsooth,
With such an one, while lordly Philip rode
By him their Turin through? But he was punished,
And must put up with—me! 'Twas sad enough
To learn my future portion and submit.
And then the wear and worry, blame on blame!
For, spring-sounds in my ears, spring-smells about,
How could I but grow dizzy in their pent
Dim palace-rooms at first? My mother's look
As they discussed my insignificance,
She and my father, and I sitting by,—
I bore; I knew how brave a son they missed;
Philip had gayly run state-papers through,
While Charles was spelling at them painfully!
But Victor was my father spite of that.
"Duke Victor's entire life has been," I said,

"Innumerable efforts to one end;
And on the point now of that end's success,
Our Ducal turning to a Kingly crown,
Where's time to be reminded 'tis his child
He spurns?" And so I suffered—scarcely suffered,
Since I had you at length!

POLYXENA
To serve in place
Of monarch, minister and mistress, Charles!

CHARLES
But, once that crown obtained, then was't not like
Our lot would alter? "When he rests, takes breath,
Glances around, sees who there's left to love—
Now that my mother's dead, sees I am left—
Is it not like he'll love me at the last?"
Well, Savoy turns Sardinia; the Duke's King:
Could I—precisely then—could you expect
His harshness to redouble? These few months
Have been ... have been ... Polyxena, do you
And God conduct me, or I lose myself!
What would he have? What is't they want with me?
Him with this mistress and this minister,
—You see me and you hear him; judge us both!
Pronounce what I should do, Polyxena!

POLYXENA
Endure, endure, beloved! Say you not
He is your father? All's so incident
To novel sway! Beside, our life must change:
Or you'll acquire his kingcraft, or he'll find
Harshness a sorry way of teaching it.
I bear this—not that there's so much to bear.

CHARLES
You bear? Do not I know that you, though bound
To silence for my sake, are perishing
Piecemeal beside me? And how otherwise
When every creephole from the hideous Court
Is stopped; the Minister to dog me, here—
The Mistress posted to entrap you, there!
And thus shall we grow old in such a life;
Not careless, never estranged,—but old: to alter
Our life, there is so much to alter!

POLYXENA
Come—

Is it agreed that we forego complaint
Even at Turin, yet complain we here
At Rivoli? 'Twere wiser you announced
Our presence to the King. What's now afoot
I wonder? Not that any more's to dread
Than every day's embarrassment: but guess
For me, why train so fast succeeded train
On the high-road, each gayer still than each!
I noticed your Archbishop's pursuivant,
The sable cloak and silver cross; such pomp
Bodes ... what now, Charles? Can you conceive?

CHARLES
Not I.

POLYXENA
A matter of some moment—

CHARLES
There's our life!
Which of the group of loiterers that stare
From the lime-avenue, divines that I—
About to figure presently, he thinks,
In face of all assembled—am the one
Who knows precisely least about it?

POLYXENA
Tush!
D'Ormea's contrivance!

CHARLES
Ay, how otherwise
Should the young Prince serve for the old King's foil?
—So that the simplest courtier may remark
'T were idle raising parties for a Prince
Content to linger the court's laughing-stock.
Something, 't is like, about that weary business

[Pointing to papers he has laid down, and which **POLYXENA** examines.

—Not that I comprehend three words, of course,
After all last night's study.

POLYXENA
The faint heart!
Why, as we rode and you rehearsed just now
Its substance ... (that 's the folded speech I mean,
Concerning the Reduction of the Fiefs)

—What would you have?—I fancied while you spoke,
Some tones were just your father's.

CHARLES
Flattery!

POLYXENA
I fancied so:—and here lurks, sure enough,
My note upon the Spanish Claims! You 've mastered
The fief-speech thoroughly: this other, mind,
Is an opinion you deliver,—stay,
Best read it slowly over once to me;
Read—there 's bare time; you read it firmly—loud
—Rather loud, looking in his face,—don't sink
Your eye once—ay, thus! "If Spain claims" ... begin
—Just as you look at me!

CHARLES
At you! Oh truly,
You have I seen, say, marshalling your troops,
Dismissing councils, or, through doors ajar,
Head sunk on hand, devoured by slow chagrins
—Then radiant, for a crown had all at once
Seemed possible again! I can behold
Him, whose least whisper ties my spirit fast,
In this sweet brow, naught could divert me from
Save objects like Sebastian's shameless lip,
Or worse, the clipped gray hair and dead white face
And dwindling eye as if it ached with guile,
D'Ormea wears ...

[As he kisses her, enter from the King's apartment **D'ORMEA**.

I said he would divert
My kisses from your brow!

D'ORMEA [Aside]
Here! So, King Victor
Spoke truth for once: and who 's ordained, but I
To make that memorable? Both in call,
As he declared! Were 't better gnash the teeth,
Or laugh outright now?

CHARLES [to **POLYXENA**]
What 's his visit for?

D'ORMEA [Aside]
I question if they even speak to me.

POLYXENA [to **CHARLES**]
Face the man! He 'll suppose you fear him else.
[Aloud] The Marquis bears the King's command, no doubt?

D'ORMEA [Aside]
Precisely!—If I threatened him, perhaps?
Well, this at least is punishment enough!
Men used to promise punishment would come.

CHARLES
Deliver the King's message, Marquis!

D'ORMEA [Aside]
Ah—
So anxious for his fate?
[Aloud] A word, my Prince,
Before you see your father—just one word
Of counsel!

CHARLES
Oh, your counsel certainly!
Polyxena, the Marquis counsels us!
Well, sir? Be brief, however!

D'ORMEA
What? You know
As much as I?—preceded me, most like,
In knowledge! So! ('T is in his eye, beside—
His voice: he knows it, and his heart 's on flame
Already!) You surmise why you, myself,
Del Borgo, Spava, fifty nobles more,
Are summoned thus?

CHARLES
Is the Prince used to know,
At any time, the pleasure of the King,
Before his minister?—Polyxena,
Stay here till I conclude my task: I feel
Your presence (smile not) through the walls, and take
Fresh heart. The King 's within that chamber?

D'ORMEA [Passing the table whereon a paper lies, exclaims, as he glances at it]
"Spain!"

POLYXENA [Aside to **CHARLES**]
Tarry awhile: what ails the minister?

D'ORMEA
Madam, I do not often trouble you.
The Prince loathes, and you scorn me—let that pass!
But since it touches him and you, not me,
Bid the Prince listen!

POLYXENA [to **CHARLES**]
Surely you will listen:
—Deceit?—Those fingers crumpling up his vest?

CHARLES
Deceitful to the very fingers' ends!

D'ORMEA [who has approached them, overlooks the other paper **CHARLES** continues to hold]
My project for the Fiefs! As I supposed!
Sir, I must give you light upon those measures
—For this is mine, and that I spied of Spain,
Mine too!

CHARLES
Release me! Do you gloze on me
Who bear in the world's face (that is, the world
You make for me at Turin) your contempt?
—Your measures?—When was not a hateful task
D'Ormea's imposition? Leave my robe!
What post can I bestow, what grant concede?
Or do you take me for the King?

D'ORMEA
Not I!
Not yet for King,—not for, as yet, thank God,
One who in ... shall I say a year, a month?
Ay!—shall be wretcheder than e'er was slave
In his Sardinia,—Europe's spectacle
And the world's by-word! What? The Prince aggrieved
That I excluded him our counsels? Here

[Touching the paper in **CHARLES'S** hand.

Accept a method of extorting gold
From Savoy's nobles, who must wring its worth
In silver first from tillers of the soil,
Whose hinds again have to contribute brass
To make up the amount: there 's counsel, sir,
My counsel, one year old; and the fruit, this—
Savoy 's become a mass of misery
And wrath, which one man has to meet—the King:
You 're not the King! Another counsel, sir!

Spain entertains a project (here it lies)
Which, guessed, makes Austria offer that same King
Thus much to baffle Spain; he promises;
Then comes Spain, breathless lest she be forestalled,
Her offer follows; and he promises ...

CHARLES
—Promises, sir, when he has just agreed
To Austria's offer?

D'ORMEA
That's a counsel, Prince!
But past our foresight, Spain and Austria (choosing
To make their quarrel up between themselves
Without the intervention of a friend)
Produce both treaties, and both promises ...

CHARLES
How?

D'ORMEA
Prince, a counsel! And the fruit of that?
Both parties covenant afresh, to fall
Together on their friend, blot out his name,
Abolish him from Europe. So, take note,
Here's Austria and here's Spain to fight against,
And what sustains the King but Savoy here,
A miserable people mad with wrongs?
You're not the King!

CHARLES
Polyxena, you said
All would clear up: all does clear up to me.

D'ORMEA
Clear up! 'T is no such thing to envy, then?
You see the King's state in its length and breadth?
You blame me now for keeping you aloof
From counsels and the fruit of counsels? Wait
Till I explain this morning's business!

CHARLES [Aside]
No—
Stoop to my father, yes,—D'Ormea, no;
—The King's son, not to the King's counsellor!
I will do something, but at least retain
The credit of my deed!
[Aloud] Then it is this

You now expressly come to tell me?

D'ORMEA
This
To tell! You apprehend me?

CHARLES
Perfectly.
Further, D'Ormea, you have shown yourself,
For the first time these many weeks and months,
Disposed to do my bidding?

D'ORMEA
From the heart!

CHARLES
Acquaint my father, first, I wait his pleasure:
Next ... or, I'll tell you at a fitter time.
Acquaint the King!

D'ORMEA [Aside]
If I 'scape Victor yet!
First, to prevent this stroke at me: if not,—
Then, to avenge it!
[To **CHARLES**] Gracious sir, I go.

[Goes.

CHARLES
God, I forbore! Which more offends, that man
Or that man's master? Is it come to this?
Have they supposed (the sharpest insult yet)
I needed e'en his intervention? No!
No—dull am I, conceded,—but so dull,
Scarcely! Their step decides me.

POLYXENA
How decides?

CHARLES
Yon would be freed D'Ormea's eye and hers?
—Could fly the court with me and live content?
So, this it is for which the knights assemble!
The whispers and the closeting of late,
The savageness and insolence of old,
—For this!

POLYXENA

What mean you?

CHARLES
How? You fail to catch
Their clever plot? I missed it, but could you?
These last two months of care to inculcate
How dull I am,—D'Ormea's present visit
To prove that, being dull, I might be worse
Were I a King—as wretched as now dull—
You recognize in it no winding up
Of a long plot?

POLYXENA
Why should there be a plot?

CHARLES
The crown's secure now; I should shame the crown—
An old complaint; the point is, how to gain
My place for one more fit in Victor's eyes,
His mistress the Sebastian's child.

POLYXENA
In truth?

CHARLES
They dare not quite dethrone Sardinia's Prince:
But they may descant on my dulness till
They sting me into even praying them
Grant leave to hide my head, resign my state,
And end the coil. Not see now? In a word,
They'd have me tender them myself my rights
As one incapable;—some cause for that,
Since I delayed thus long to see their drift!
I shall apprise the King he may resume
My rights this moment.

POLYXENA
Pause! I dare not think
So ill of Victor.

CHARLES
Think no ill of him!

POLYXENA
—Nor think him, then, so shallow as to suffer
His purpose be divined thus easily.
And yet—you are the last of a great line;
There's a great heritage at stake; new days

Seemed to await this newest of the realms
Of Europe:—Charles, you must withstand this!

CHARLES
Ah!
You dare not then renounce the splendid court
For one whom all the world despises? Speak!

POLYXENA

My gentle husband, speak I will, and truth.
Were this as you believe, and I once sure
Your duty lay in so renouncing rule,
I could ... could? Oh what happiness it were
To live, my Charles, and die, alone with you!

CHARLES

I grieve I asked you. To the presence, then!
By this, D'Ormea acquaints the King, no doubt,
He fears I am too simple for mere hints,
And that no less will serve than Victor's mouth
Demonstrating in council what I am.
I have not breathed, I think, these many years!

POLYXENA

Why, it may be!—if he desire to wed
That woman, call legitimate her child.

CHARLES

You see as much? Oh, let his will have way!
You'll not repent confiding in me, love?
There's many a brighter spot in Piedmont, far,
Than Rivoli. I'll seek him: or, suppose
You hear first how I mean to speak my mind?
Loudly and firmly both, this time, be sure!
I yet may see your Rhine-land, who can tell?
Once away, ever then away! I breathe.

POLYXENA
And I too breathe.

CHARLES
Come, my Polyxena!

KING VICTOR

PART II

Enter **KING VICTOR**, bearing the regalia on a cushion, from his apartment. He calls loudly—

D'Ormea!—for patience fails me, treading thus
Among the obscure trains I have laid,—my knights
Safe in the hall here—in that anteroom,
My son,—D'Ormea, where? Of this, one touch—

[Laying down the crown.

This fireball to these mute black cold trains—then
Outbreak enough!

[Contemplating it.

To lose all, after all!
This, glancing o'er my house for ages—shaped,
Brave meteor, like the crown of Cyprus now,
Jerusalem, Spain, England, every change
The braver,—and when I have clutched a prize
My ancestry died wan with watching for,
To lose it!—by a slip, a fault, a trick
Learnt to advantage once and not unlearned
When past the use,—"just this once more" (I thought)
"Use it with Spain and Austria happily,
And then away with trick!" An oversight
I'd have repaired thrice over, any time
These fifty years, must happen now! There 's peace
At length; and I, to make the most of peace,
Ventured my project on our people here,
As needing not their help: which Europe knows,
And means, cold-blooded, to dispose herself
(Apart from plausibilities of war)
To crush the new-made King—who ne'er till now
Feared her. As Duke, I lost each foot of earth
And laughed at her: my name was left, my sword
Left, all was left! But she can take, she knows,
This crown, herself conceded ...
That's to try,
Kind Europe!—My career's not closed as yet,
This boy was ever subject to my will,
Timid and tame—the fitter!—D'Ormea, too
What if the sovereign also rid himself
Of thee, his prime of parasites? I delay!
D'Ormea!

[As **D'ORMEA** enters, the **KING** seats himself.

My son, the Prince—attends he?

D'ORMEA
Sir,
He does attend. The crown prepared!—it seems
That you persist in your resolve.

VICTOR
Who's come?
The chancellor and the chamberlain? My knights?

D'ORMEA
The whole Annunziata. If, my liege,
Your fortune had not tottered worse than now ...

VICTOR
Del Borgo has drawn up the schedules? mine—
My son's, too? Excellent! Only, beware
Of the least blunder, or we look but fools.
First, you read the Annulment of the Oaths;
Del Borgo follows ... no, the Prince shall sign;
Then let Del Borgo read the Instrument:
On which, I enter.

D'ORMEA
Sir, this may be truth;
You, sir, may do as you affect—may break
Your engine, me, to pieces: try at least
If not a spring remain worth saving! Take
My counsel as I've counselled many times!
What if the Spaniard and the Austrian threat?
There 's England, Holland, Venice—which ally
Select you?

VICTOR
Aha! Come, D'Ormea,—"truth"
Was on your lip a minute since. Allies?
I've broken faith with Venice, Holland, England
—As who knows if not you?

D'ORMEA
But why with me
Break faith—with one ally, your best, break faith?

VICTOR
When first I stumbled on you, Marquis—'t was
At Mondovi—a little lawyer's clerk ...

D'ORMEA

Therefore your soul's ally!—who brought you through
Your quarrel with the Pope, at pains enough—
Who simply echoed you in these affairs—
On whom you cannot therefore visit these
Affairs' ill fortune—whom you trust to guide
You safe (yes, on my soul) through these affairs!

VICTOR

I was about to notice, had you not
Prevented me, that since that great town kept
With its chicane D'Ormea's satchel stuffed
And D'Ormea's self sufficiently recluse,
He missed a sight,—my naval armament
When I burned Toulon. How the skiff exults
Upon the galliot's wave!—rises its height,
O'ertops it even; but the great wave bursts,
And hell-deep in the horrible profound
Buries itself the galliot: shall the skiff
Think to escape the sea's black trough in turn?
Apply this: you have been my minister
—Next me, above me possibly;—sad post,
Huge care, abundant lack of peace of mind;
Who would desiderate the eminence?
You gave your soul to get it; you'd yet give
Your soul to keep it, as I mean you shall,
D'Ormea! What if the wave ebbed with me?
Whereas it cants you to another crest;
I toss you to my son; ride out your ride!

D'ORMEA

Ah, you so much despise me?

VICTOR

You, D'Ormea?
Nowise: and I'll inform you why. A king
Must in his time have many ministers,
And I've been rash enough to part with mine
When I thought proper. Of the tribe, not one
(... Or wait, did Pianezze? ... ah, just the same!)
Not one of them, ere his remonstrance reached
The length of yours, but has assured me (commonly
Standing much as you stand,—or nearer, say,
The door to make his exit on his speech)
—I should repent of what I did. D'Ormea,
Be candid, you approached it when I bade you
Prepare the schedules! But you stopped in time,
You have not so assured me: how should I

Despise you then?

[Enter **CHARLES**.

VICTOR [Changing his tone]
Are you instructed? Do
My order, point by point! About it, sir!

D'ORMEA
You so despise me!
[Aside] One last stay remains—
The boy's discretion there.
[To **CHARLES**]
For your sake, Prince,
I pleaded, wholly in your interest,
To save you from this fate!

CHARLES [Aside]
Must I be told
The Prince was supplicated for—by him?

VICTOR [To **D'ORMEA**]
Apprise Del Borgo, Spava, and the rest,
Our son attends them; then return.

D'ORMEA
One word!

CHARLES [Aside]
A moment's pause and they would drive me hence,
I do believe!

D'ORMEA [Aside]
Let but the boy be firm!

VICTOR
You disobey?

CHARLES [To **D'ORMEA**]
You do not disobey
Me, at least. Did you promise that or no?

D'ORMEA
Sir, I am yours: what would you? Yours am I!

CHARLES
When I have said what I shall say, 't is like
Your face will ne'er again disgust me. Go!

Through you, as through a breast of glass, I see.
And for your conduct, from my youth till now,
Take my contempt! You might have spared me much,
Secured me somewhat, nor so harmed yourself:
That's over now. Go, ne'er to come again!

D'ORMEA
As son, the father—father, as the son!
My wits! My wits!

[Goes.

VICTOR [Seated]
And you, what meant you, pray,
Speaking thus to D'Ormea?

CHARLES
Let us not
Waste words upon D'Ormea! Those I spent
Have half unsettled what I came to say.
His presence vexes to my very soul.

VICTOR
One called to manage a kingdom, Charles, needs heart
To bear up under worse annoyances
Than seems D'Ormea—to me, at least.

CHARLES [Aside]
Ah, good!
He keeps me to the point! Then be it so.
[Aloud] Last night, sir, brought me certain papers—these—
To be reported on,—your way of late.
Is it last night's result that you demand?

VICTOR
For God's sake, what has night brought forth? Pronounce
The ... what 's your word?—result!

CHARLES
Sir, that had proved
Quite worthy of your sneer, no doubt:—a few
Lame thoughts, regard for you alone could wring,
Lame as they are, from brains like mine, believe!
As 't is, sir, I am spared both toil and sneer.
These are the papers.

VICTOR
Well, sir? I suppose

You hardly burned them. Now for your result!

CHARLES
I never should have done great things, of course,
But ... oh my father, had you loved me more!

VICTOR
Loved? [Aside] Has D'Ormea played me false, I wonder?
[Aloud] Why, Charles, a king's love is diffused—yourself
May overlook, perchance, your part in it.
Our monarchy is absolutest now
In Europe, or my trouble's thrown away.
I love, my mode, that subjects each and all
May have the power of loving, all and each,
Their mode: I doubt not, many have their sons
To trifle with, talk soft to, all day long:
I have that crown, this chair, D'Ormea, Charles!

CHARLES
'T is well I am a subject then, not you.

VICTOR [Aside]
D'Ormea has told him everything.
[Aloud] Aha,
I apprehend you: when all 's said, you take
Your private station to be prized beyond
My own, for instance?

CHARLES
—Do and ever did
So take it: 't is the method you pursue
That grieves ...

VICTOR
These words! Let me express, my friend,
Your thoughts. You penetrate what I supposed
Secret. D'Ormea plies his trade betimes!
I purpose to resign my crown to you.

CHARLES
To me?

VICTOR
Now,—in that chamber.

CHARLES
You resign
The crown to me?

VICTOR

And time enough, Charles, sure?
Confess with me, at four-and-sixty years
A crown 's a load. I covet quiet once
Before I die, and summoned you for that.

CHARLES

'T is I will speak: you ever hated me,
I bore it,—have insulted me, borne too—
Now you insult yourself; and I remember
What I believed you, what you really are,
And cannot bear it. What! My life has passed
Under your eye, tormented as you know,—
Your whole sagacities, one after one,
At leisure brought to play on me—to prove me
A fool, I thought and I submitted; now
You'd prove ... what would you prove me?

VICTOR

This to me?
I hardly know you!

CHARLES

Know me? Oh indeed
You do not! Wait till I complain next time
Of my simplicity!—for here 's a sage
Knows the world well, is not to be deceived,
And his experience and his Macchiavels,
D'Ormeas, teach him—what?—that I this while
Have envied him his crown! He has not smiled,
I warrant,—has not eaten, drunk, nor slept,
For I was plotting with my Princess yonder!
Who knows what we might do or might not do?
Go now, be politic, astound the world!
That sentry in the antechamber—nay,
The varlet who disposed this precious trap

[Pointing to the crown.

That was to take me—ask them if they think
Their own sons envy them their posts!—Know me!

VICTOR

But you know me, it seems: so, learn, in brief,
My pleasure. This assembly is convened ...

CHARLES

Tell me, that woman put it in your head!
You were not sole contriver of the scheme,
My father!

VICTOR
Now observe me, sir! I jest
Seldom—on these points, never. Here, I say,
The knights assemble to see me concede,
And you accept, Sardinia's crown.

CHARLES
Farewell!
'T were vain to hope to change this: I can end it.
Not that I cease from being yours, when sunk
Into obscurity: I 'll die for you,
But not annoy you with my presence. Sir,
Farewell! Farewell!

[Enter **D'ORMEA**.

D'ORMEA [Aside]
Ha, sure he's changed again—
Means not to fall into the cunning trap!
Then, Victor, I shall yet escape you, Victor!

VICTOR [Suddenly placing the crown upon the head of **CHARLES**]
D'Ormea, your king!
[To **CHARLES**]
My son, obey me! Charles,
Your father, clearer-sighted than yourself,
Decides it must be so. 'Faith, this looks real!
My reasons after; reason upon reason
After: but now, obey me! Trust in me!
By this, you save Sardinia, you save me!
Why, the boy swoons!
[To **D'ORMEA**]
Come this side!

D'ORMEA [As **CHARLES** turns from him to **VICTOR**]
You persist?

VICTOR
Yes, I conceive the gesture's meaning. 'Faith,
He almost seems to hate you: how is that?
Be reassured, my Charles! Is 't over now?
Then, Marquis, tell the new King what remains
To do! A moment's work. Del Borgo reads
The Act of Abdication out, you sign it,

Then I sign; after that, come back to me.

D'ORMEA
Sir, for the last time, pause!

VICTOR
Five minutes longer
I am your sovereign, Marquis. Hesitate—
And I 'll so turn those minutes to account
That ... Ay, you recollect me!
[Aside] Could I bring
My foolish mind to undergo the reading
That Act of Abdication!

[As **CHARLES** motions **D'ORMEA** to precede him.

Thanks, dear Charles!

[**CHARLES** and **D'ORMEA** retire.

VICTOR
A novel feature in the boy,—indeed
Just what I feared he wanted most. Quite right,
This earnest tone: your truth, now for effect!
It answers every purpose: with that look,
That voice,—I hear him: "I began no treaty,"
(He speaks to Spain,) "nor ever dreamed of this
You show me; this I from my soul regret;
But if my father signed it, bid not me
Dishonor him—who gave me all, beside:"
And, "true," says Spain, "'t were harsh to visit that
Upon the Prince." Then come the nobles trooping:
"I grieve at these exactions—I had cut
This hand off ere impose them; but shall I
Undo my father's deed?"—and they confer:
"Doubtless he was no party, after all;
Give the Prince time!"
Ay, give us time, but time!
Only, he must not, when the dark day comes,
Refer our friends to me and frustrate all.
We 'll have no child's play, no desponding fits,
No Charles at each cross turn entreating Victor
To take his crown again. Guard against that!

[Enter **D'ORMEA**.

Long live King Charles!
No—Charles's counsellor!

Well, is it over, Marquis? Did I jest?

D'ORMEA
"King Charles!" What then may you be?

VICTOR
Anything!
A country gentleman that, cured of bustle,
Now beats a quick retreat toward Chambery,
Would hunt and hawk and leave you noisy folk
To drive your trade without him. I'm Count Remont—
Count Tende—any little place's Count!

D'ORMEA
Then Victor, Captain against Catinat
At Staffarde, where the French beat you; and Duke
At Turin, where you beat the French; King late
Of Savoy, Piedmont, Montferrat, Sardinia,
—Now, "any little place's Count"—

VICTOR
Proceed!

D'ORMEA
Breaker of vows to God, who crowned you first;
Breaker of vows to man, who kept you since;
Most profligate to me who outraged God
And man to serve you, and am made pay crimes
I was but privy to, by passing thus
To your imbecile son—who, well you know,
Must—(when the people here, and nations there,
Clamor for you the main delinquent, slipped
From King to—"Count of any little place)"
Must needs surrender me, all in his reach,—
I, sir, forgive you: for I see the end—
See you on your return—(you will return)—
To him you trust, a moment ...

VICTOR
Trust him? How?
My poor man, merely a prime-minister,
Make me know where my trust errs!

D'ORMEA
In his fear,
His love, his—but discover for yourself
What you are weakest, trusting in!

VICTOR

Aha,
D'Ormea, not a shrewder scheme than this
In your repertory? You know old Victor—
Vain, choleric, inconstant, rash—(I 've heard
Talkers who little thought the King so close)—
Felicitous now, were 't not, to provoke him
To clean forget, one minute afterward,
His solemn act, and call the nobles back
And pray them give again the very power
He has abjured?—for the dear sake of what?
Vengeance on you, D'Ormea! No: such am I,
Count Tende or Count anything you please,
—Only, the same that did the things you say,
And, among other things you say not, used
Your finest fibre, meanest muscle,—you
I used, and now, since you will have it so,
Leave to your fate—mere lumber in the midst,
You and your works. Why, what on earth beside
Are you made for, you sort of ministers?

D'ORMEA

Not left, though, to my fate! Your witless son
Has more wit than to load himself with lumber:
He foils you that way, and I follow you.

VICTOR

Stay with my son—protect the weaker side!

D'ORMEA

Ay, to be tossed the people like a rag,
And flung by them for Spain and Austria's sport,
Abolishing the record of your part
In all this perfidy!

VICTOR

Prevent, beside,
My own return!

D'ORMEA

That's half prevented now!
'Twill go hard but you find a wondrous charm
In exile, to discredit me. The Alps,
Silk-mills to watch, vines asking vigilance—
Hounds open for the stag, your hawk's a-wing—
Brave days that wait the Louis of the South,
Italy's Janus!

VICTOR
So, the lawyer's clerk
Won't tell me that I shall repent!

D'ORMEA
You give me
Full leave to ask if you repent?

VICTOR
Whene'er
Sufficient time's elapsed for that, you judge!

[Shouts inside, "KING CHARLES!"

D'ORMEA
Do you repent?

VICTOR [After a slight pause]
… I've kept them waiting? Yes!
Come in, complete the Abdication, sir!

[They go out.

[Enter **POLYXENA**.

POLYXENA
A shout! The sycophants are free of Charles!
Oh, is not this like Italy? No fruit
Of his or my distempered fancy, this,
But just an ordinary fact! Beside,
Here they've set forms for such proceedings; Victor
Imprisoned his own mother: he should know,
If any, how a son's to be deprived
Of a son's right. Our duty's palpable.
Ne'er was my husband for the wily king
And the unworthy subjects: be it so!
Come you safe out of them, my Charles! Our life
Grows not the broad and dazzling life, I dreamed
Might prove your lot; for strength was shut in you
None guessed but I—strength which, untrammelled once,
Had little shamed your vaunted ancestry—
Patience and self-devotion, fortitude,
Simplicity and utter truthfulness
—All which, they shout to lose!
So, now my work
Begins—to save him from regret. Save Charles
Regret?—the noble nature! He's not made
Like these Italians: 'tis a German soul.

[**CHARLES** enters crowned.

Oh, where's the King's heir? Gone:—the Crown-prince? Gone:—
Where's Savoy? Gone!—Sardinia? Gone! But Charles
Is left! And when my Rhine-land bowers arrive,
If he looked almost handsome yester-twilight
As his gray eyes seemed widening into black
Because I praised him, then how will he look?
Farewell, you stripped and whited mulberry-trees
Bound each to each by lazy ropes of vine!
Now I'll teach you my language: I'm not forced
To speak Italian now, Charles?

[She sees the crown.

What is this?
Answer me—who has done this? Answer!

CHARLES
He!
I am King now.

POLYXENA
Oh worst, worst, worst of all!
Tell me! What, Victor? He has made you King?
What 's he then? What 's to follow this? You, King?

CHARLES
Have I done wrong? Yes, for you were not by!

POLYXENA
Tell me from first to last.

CHARLES
Hush—a new world
Brightens before me; he is moved away
—The dark form that eclipsed it, he subsides
Into a shape supporting me like you,
And I, alone, tend upward, more and more
Tend upward: I am grown Sardinia's King.

POLYXENA
Now stop: was not this Victor, Duke of Savoy
At ten years old?

CHARLES
He was.

POLYXENA

And the Duke spent,
Since then, just four-and-fifty years in toil
To be—what?

CHARLES

King.

POLYXENA

Then why unking himself?

CHARLES

Those years are cause enough.

POLYXENA

The only cause?

CHARLES

Some new perplexities.

POLYXENA

Which you can solve
Although he cannot?

CHARLES

He assures me so.

POLYXENA

And this he means shall last—how long?

CHARLES

How long?
Think you I fear the perils I confront?
He's praising me before the people's face—
My people!

POLYXENA

Then he's changed—grown kind, the King?
Where can the trap be?

CHARLES

Heart and soul I pledge!
My father, could I guard the crown you gained,
Transmit as I received it,—all good else
Would I surrender!

POLYXENA

Ah, it opens then
Before you, all you dreaded formerly?
You are rejoiced to be a king, my Charles?

CHARLES
So much to dare? The better,—much to dread;
The better. I'll adventure though alone.
Triumph or die, there 's Victor still to witness
Who dies or triumphs—either way, alone!

POLYXENA
Once I had found my share in triumph, Charles,
Or death.

CHARLES
But you are I! But you I call
To take, Heaven's proxy, vows I tendered Heaven
A moment since. I will deserve the crown!

POLYXENA
You will. [Aside] No doubt it were a glorious thing
For any people, if a heart like his
Ruled over it. I would I saw the trap.

[Enter **VICTOR**.

'T is he must show me.

VICTOR
So, the mask falls off
An old man's foolish love at last. Spare thanks!
I know you, and Polyxena I know.
Here's Charles—I am his guest now—does he bid me
Be seated? And my light-haired blue-eyed child
Must not forget the old man far away
At Chambery, who dozes while she reigns.

POLYXENA
Most grateful shall we now be, talking least
Of gratitude—indeed of anything
That hinders what yourself must need to say
To Charles.

CHARLES
Pray speak, sir!

VICTOR
'Faith, not much to say:

Only what shows itself, you once i' the point
Of sight. You're now the King: you 'll comprehend
Much you may oft have wondered at—the shifts,
Dissimulation, wiliness I showed.
For what's our post? Here 's Savoy and here 's Piedmont,
Here's Montferrat—a breadth here, a space there—
To o'er-sweep all these, what 's one weapon worth?
I often think of how they fought in Greece
(Or Rome, which was it? You 're the scholar, Charles!)
You made a front-thrust? But if your shield too
Were not adroitly planted, some shrewd knave
Reached you behind; and him foiled, straight if thong
And handle of that shield were not cast loose,
And you enabled to outstrip the wind,
Fresh foes assailed you, either side; 'scape these,
And reach your place of refuge—e'en then, odds
If the gate opened unless breath enough
Were left in you to make its lord a speech.
Oh, you will see!

CHARLES
No: straight on shall I go,
Truth helping; win with it or die with it.

VICTOR
'Faith, Charles, you're not made Europe's fighting-man!
The barrier-guarder, if you please. You clutch
Hold and consolidate, with envious France
This side, with Austria that, the territory
I held—ay, and will hold ... which you shall hold
Despite the couple! But I've surely earned
Exemption from these weary politics,
—The privilege to prattle with my son
And daughter here, though Europe wait the while.

POLYXENA
Nay, sir,—at Chambery, away forever,
As soon you will be, 't is farewell we bid you:
Turn these few fleeting moments to account!
'T is just as though it were a death.

VICTOR
Indeed!

POLYXENA [Aside]
Is the trap there?

CHARLES

Ay, call this parting—death!
The sacreder your memory becomes.
If I misrule Sardinia, how bring back
My father?

VICTOR
I mean...

POLYXENA [who watches **VICTOR** narrowly this while]
Your father does not mean
You should be ruling for your father's sake:
It is your people must concern you wholly
Instead of him. You mean this, sir? (He drops
My hand!)

CHARLES
That people is now part of me.

VICTOR
About the people! I took certain measures
Some short time since ... Oh, I know well, you know
But little of my measures! These affect
The nobles; we've resumed some grants, imposed
A tax or two: prepare yourself, in short,
For clamor on that score. Mark me: you yield
No jot of aught entrusted you!

POLYXENA
No jot
You yield!

CHARLES
My father, when I took the oath,
Although my eye might stray in search of yours,
I heard it, understood it, promised God
What you require. Till from this eminence
He move me, here I keep, nor shall concede
The meanest of my rights.

VICTOR [Aside]
The boy's a fool!
—Or rather, I'm a fool: for, what's wrong here?
To-day the sweets of reigning: let to-morrow
Be ready with its bitters.

[Enter **D'ORMEA**.

There 's beside

Somewhat to press upon your notice first.

CHARLES
Then why delay it for an instant, sir?
That Spanish claim perchance? And, now you speak,
—This morning, my opinion was mature,
Which, boy-like, I was bashful in producing
To one I ne'er am like to fear in future!
My thought is formed upon that Spanish claim.

VICTOR
Betimes indeed. Not now, Charles! You require
A host of papers on it.

D'ORMEA [Coming forward]
Here they are.
[To **CHARLES**]
I, sir, was minister and much beside
Of the late monarch; to say little, him
I served: on you I have, to say e'en less.
No claim. This case contains those papers: with them
I tender you my office.

VICTOR [Hastily]
Keep him, Charles!
There's reason for it—many reasons: you
Distrust him, nor are so far-wrong there,—but
He's mixed up in this matter—he'll desire
To quit you, for occasions known to me:
Do not accept those reasons: have him stay!

POLYXENA [Aside]
His minister thrust on us!

CHARLES [To **D'ORMEA**]
Sir, believe,
In justice to myself, you do not need
E'en this commending: howsoe'er might seem
My feelings toward you, as a private man,
They quit me in the vast and untried field
Of action. Though I shall myself (as late
In your own hearing I engaged to do)
Preside o'er my Sardinia, yet your help
Is necessary. Think the past forgotten
And serve me now!

D'ORMEA
I did not offer you

My service—would that I could serve you, sir!
As for the Spanish matter ...

VICTOR
But dispatch
At least the dead, in my good daughter's phrase,
Before the living! Help to house me safe
Ere with D'Ormea you set the world agape!
Here is a paper—will you overlook
What I propose reserving for my needs?
I get as far from you as possible:
Here 's what I reckon my expenditure.

CHARLES [Reading]
A miserable fifty thousand crowns!

VICTOR
Oh, quite enough for country gentlemen!
Beside, the exchequer happens ... but find out
All that, yourself!

CHARLES [Still reading]
"Count Tende"—what means this?

VICTOR
Me: you were but an infant when I burst
Through the defile of Tende upon France.
Had only my allies kept true to me!
No matter. Tende's, then, a name I take
Just as ...

D'ORMEA
—The Marchioness Sebastian takes
The name of Spigno.

CHARLES
How, sir?

VICTOR [To **D'ORMEA**]
Fool! All that
Was for my own detailing.
[To **CHARLES**] That anon!

CHARLES [To **D'ORMEA**]
Explain what you have said, sir!

D'ORMEA
I supposed

The marriage of the King to her I named,
Profoundly kept a secret these few weeks,
Was not to be one, now he's Count.

POLYXENA [Aside]
With us
The minister—with him the mistress!

CHARLES [To **VICTOR**]
No—
Tell me you have not taken her—that woman—
To live with, past recall!

VICTOR
And where 's the crime ...

POLYXENA [To **CHARLES**]
True, sir, this is a matter past recall
And past your cognizance. A day before,
And you had been compelled to note this—now
Why note it? The King saved his House from shame:
What the Count did, is no concern of yours.

CHARLES [After a pause]
The Spanish claim, D'Ormea!

VICTOR
Why, my son,
I took some ill-advised ... one's age, in fact,
Spoils everything: though I was overreached,
A younger brain, we 'll trust, may extricate
Sardinia readily. To-morrow, D'Ormea,
Inform the King!

D'ORMEA [Without regarding **VICTOR**, and leisurely]
Thus stands the ease with Spain:
When first the Infant Carlos claimed his proper
Succession to the throne of Tuscany ...

VICTOR
I tell you, that stands over! Let that rest!
There is the policy!

CHARLES [To **D'ORMEA**]
Thus much I know,
And more—too much. The remedy?

D'ORMEA

Of course!
No glimpse of one.

VICTOR
No remedy at all!
It makes the remedy itself—time makes it.

D'ORMEA [To **CHARLES**]
But if ...

VICTOR [Still more hastily]
In fine, I shall take care of that:
And, with another project that I have ...

D'ORMEA [Turning on him]
Oh, since Count Tende means to take again
King Victor's crown!—

POLYXENA [Throwing herself at **VICTOR'S** feet]
E'en now retake it, sir!
Oh, speak! We are your subjects both, once more!
Say it—a word effects it! You meant not,
Nor do mean now, to take it: but you must!
'T is in you—in your nature—and the shame 's
Not half the shame 't would grow to afterwards!

CHARLES
Polyxena!

POLYXENA
A word recalls the knights—
Say it!—What 's promising and what 's the past?
Say you are still King Victor!

D'ORMEA
Better say
The Count repents, in brief!

[**VICTOR** rises.

CHARLES
With such a crime
I have not charged you, sir!

POLYXENA
Charles turns from me!

PART I

Enter **QUEEN POLYXENA** and **D'ORMEA.**—A pause.

POLYXENA
And now, sir, what have you to say?

D'ORMEA
Count Tende ...

POLYXENA
Affirm not I betrayed you; you resolve
On uttering this strange intelligence
—Nay, post yourself to find me ere I reach
The capital, because you know King Charles
Tarries a day or two at Evian baths
Behind me:—but take warning,—here and thus

[Seating herself in the royal seat.

I listen, if I listen—not your friend.
Explicitly the statement, if you still
Persist to urge it on me, must proceed:
I am not made for aught else.

D'ORMEA
Good! Count Tende ...

POLYXENA
I, who mistrust you, shall acquaint King Charles,
Who even more mistrusts you.

D'ORMEA
Does he so?

POLYXENA
Why should he not?

D'ORMEA
Ay, why not? Motives, seek
You virtuous people, motives! Say, I serve
God at the devil's bidding—will that do?
I 'm proud: our people have been pacified,
Really I know not how—

POLYXENA
By truthfulness.

D'ORMEA
Exactly; that shows I had naught to do
With pacifying them. Our foreign perils
Also exceed my means to stay: but here
'T is otherwise, and my pride 's piqued. Count Tende
Completes a full year's absence: would you, madam,
Have the old monarch back, his mistress back,
His measures back? I pray you, act upon
My counsel, or they will be.

POLYXENA
When?

D'ORMEA
Let 's think.
Home-matters settled—Victor 's coming now;
Let foreign matters settle—Victor 's here
Unless I stop him; as I will, this way.

POLYXENA [Reading the papers he presents]
If this should prove a plot 'twixt you and Victor?
You seek annoyances to give the pretext
For what you say you fear!

D'ORMEA
Oh, possibly!
I go for nothing. Only show King Charles
That thus Count Tende purposes return,
And style me his inviter, if you please!

POLYXENA
Half of your tale is true; most like, the Count
Seeks to return: but why stay you with us?
To aid in such emergencies.

D'ORMEA
Keep safe
Those papers: or, to serve me, leave no proof
I thus have counselled! When the Count returns,
And the King abdicates, 't will stead me little
To have thus counselled.

POLYXENA
The King abdicate!

D'ORMEA

He 's good, we knew long since—wise, we discover—
Firm, let us hope:—but I 'd have gone to work
With him away. Well!

[**CHARLES** without.
In the Council Chamber?

D'ORMEA

All 's lost!

POLYXENA

Oh, surely not King Charles! He 's changed—
That 's not this year's care-burdened voice and step:
'T is last year's step, the Prince's voice!

D'ORMEA

I know.

[Enter **CHARLES** —**D'ORMEA** retiring a little.

CHARLES

Now wish me joy, Polyxena! Wish it me
The old way!

[She embraces him.

There was too much cause for that!
But I have found myself again. What news
At Turin? Oh, if you but felt the load
I 'm free of—free! I said this year would end
Or it, or me—but I am free, thank God!

POLYXENA

How, Charles?

CHARLES

You do not guess? The day I found
Sardinia's hideous coil, at home, abroad,
And how my father was involved in it,—
Of course, I vowed to rest and smile no more
Until I cleared his name from obloquy.
We did the people right—'t was much to gain
That point, redress our nobles' grievance, too—
But that took place here, was no crying shame:
All must be done abroad,—if I abroad
Appeased the justly-angered Powers, destroyed
The scandal, took down Victor's name at last

From a bad eminence, I then might breathe
And rest! No moment was to lose. Behold
The proud result—a Treaty, Austria, Spain
Agree to—

D'ORMEA [Aside]
I shall merely stipulate
For an experienced headsman.

CHARLES
Not a soul
Is compromised: the blotted past 's a blank:
Even D'Ormea escapes unquestioned. See!
It reached me from Vienna; I remained
At Evian to dispatch the Count his news;
'T is gone to Chambery a week ago—
And here am I: do I deserve to feel
Your warm white arms around me?

D'ORMEA [Coming forward]
He knows that?

CHARLES
What, in Heaven's name, means this?

D'ORMEA
He knows that matters
Are settled at Vienna? Not too late!
Plainly, unless you post this very hour
Some man you trust (say, me) to Chambery
And take precautions I acquaint you with,
Your father will return here.

CHARLES
Are you crazed,
D'Ormea? Here? For what? As well return
To take his crown!

D'ORMEA
He will return for that.

CHARLES [To **POLYXENA**]
You have not listened to this man?

POLYXENA
He spoke
About your safety—and I listened.

[He disengages himself from her arms.

CHARLES [To **D'ORMEA**]
What
Apprised you of the Count's intentions?

D'ORMEA
Me?
His heart, sir; you may not be used to read
Such evidence however; therefore read

[Pointing to **POLYXENA'S** papers.

My evidence.

CHARLES [To **POLYXENA**]
Oh, worthy this of you!
And of your speech I never have forgotten,
Though I professed forgetfulness; which haunts me
As if I did not know how false it was;
Which made me toil unconsciously thus long
That there might be no least occasion left
For aught of its prediction coming true!
And now, when there is left no least occasion
To instigate my father to such crime—
When I might venture to forget (I hoped)
That speech and recognize Polyxena—
Oh worthy, to revive, and tenfold worse,
That plague! D'Ormea at your ear, his slanders
Still in your hand! Silent?

POLYXENA
As the wronged are.

CHARLES
And you, D'Ormea, since when have you presumed
To spy upon my father? I conceive
What that wise paper shows, and easily.
Since when?

D'ORMEA
The when and where and how belong
To me. 'T is sad work, but I deal in such.
You ofttimes serve yourself; I'd serve you here:
Use makes me not so squeamish. In a word,
Since the first hour he went to Chambery,
Of his seven servants, five have I suborned.

CHARLES
You hate my father?

D'ORMEA
Oh, just as you will!

[Looking at **POLYXENA**.

A minute since, I loved him—hate him, now!
What matter?—if you ponder just one thing:
Has he that treaty?—he is setting forward
Already. Are your guards here?

CHARLES
Well for you
They are not!
[To **POLYXENA**]
Him I knew of old, but you—
To hear that pickthank, further his designs!
[To **D'ORMEA**]
Guards?—were they here, I 'd bid them, for your trouble,
Arrest you.

D'ORMEA
Guards you shall not want. I lived
The servant of your choice, not of your need.
You never greatly needed me till now
That you discard me. This is my arrest.
Again I tender you my charge—its duty
Would bid me press you read those documents.
Here, sir!

[Offering his badge of Office.

CHARLES [Taking it]
The papers also! Do you think
I dare not read them?

POLYXENA
Read them, sir!

CHARLES
They prove,
My father, still a month within the year
Since he so solemnly consigned it me,
Means to resume his crown? They shall prove that,
Or my best dungeon ...

D'ORMEA
Even say, Chambery!
'T is vacant, I surmise, by this.

CHARLES
You prove
Your words or pay their forfeit, sir. Go there!
Polyxena, one chance to rend the veil
Thickening and blackening 'twixt us two! Do say,
You 'll see the falsehood of the charges proved!
Do say, at least, you wish to see them proved
False charges—my heart's love of other times!

POLYXENA
Ah, Charles!

CHARLES [To **D'ORMEA**]
Precede me, sir!

D'ORMEA
And I 'm at length
A martyr for the truth! No end, they say,
Of miracles. My conscious innocence!

[As they go out, enter—by the middle door, at which he pauses—**VICTOR**.

VICTOR
Sure I heard voices? No. Well, I do best
To make at once for this, the heart o' the place.
The old room! Nothing changed! So near my seat,
D'Ormea?

[Pushing away the stool which is by the **KING'S** chair.

I want that meeting over first,
I know not why. Tush, he, D'Ormea, slow
To hearten me, the supple knave? That burst
Of spite so eased him! He 'll inform me ...
What?
Why come I hither? All 's in rough: let all
Remain rough. There 's full time to draw back—nay,
There 's naught to draw back from, as yet; whereas,
If reason should be, to arrest a course
Of error—reason good, to interpose
And save, as I have saved so many times,
Our House, admonish my son's giddy youth,
Relieve him of a weight that proves too much—
Now is the time,—or now, or never.

'Faith,
This kind of step is pitiful, not due
To Charles, this stealing back—hither, because
He 's from his capital! Oh Victor! Victor!
But thus it is. The age of crafty men
Is loathsome; youth contrives to carry off
Dissimulation; we may intersperse
Extenuating passages of strength,
Ardor, vivacity and wit—may turn
E'en guile into a voluntary grace:
But one's old age, when graces drop away
And leave guile the pure staple of our lives—
Ah, loathsome!
Not so—or why pause I? Turin
Is mine to have, were I so minded, for
The asking; all the army 's mine—I 've witnessed
Each private fight beneath me; all the Court 's
Mine too; and, best of all, D'Ormea's still
D'Ormea and mine. There 's some grace clinging yet.
Had I decided on this step, ere midnight
I 'd take the crown.
No. Just this step to rise
Exhausts me. Here am I arrived: the rest
Must be done for me. Would I could sit here
And let things right themselves, the masque unmasque
Of the old King, crownless, gray hair and hot blood,—
The young King, crowned, but calm before his time,
They say,—the eager mistress with her taunts,—
And the sad earnest wife who motions me
Away—ay, there she knelt to me! E'en yet
I can return and sleep at Chambery
A dream out.
Rather shake it off at Turin,
King Victor! Say: to Turin—yes, or no?
'T is this relentless noonday-lighted chamber.
Lighted like life but silent as the grave,
That disconcerts me. That 's the change must strike.
No silence last year! Some one flung doors wide
(Those two great doors which scrutinize me now)
And out I went 'mid crowds of men—men talking,
Men watching if my lip fell or brow knit,
Men saw me safe forth, put me on my road:
That makes the misery of this return.
Oh had a battle done it! Had I dropped,
Haling some battle, three entire days old,
Hither and thither by the forehead—dropped
In Spain, in Austria, best of all, in France—
Spurned on its horns or underneath its hoofs,

When the spent monster went upon its knees
To pad and pash the prostrate wretch—I, Victor,
Sole to have stood up against France, beat down
By inches, brayed to pieces finally
In some vast unimaginable charge,
A flying hell of horse and foot and guns
Over me, and all 's lost, forever lost,
There 's no more Victor when the world wakes up!
Then silence, as of a raw battlefield,
Throughout the world. Then after (as whole days
After, you catch at intervals faint noise
Through the stiff crust of frozen blood)—there creeps
A rumor forth, so faint, no noise at all,
That a strange old man, with face outworn for wounds,
Is stumbling on from frontier town to town,
Begging a pittance that may help him find
His Turin out; what scorn and laughter follow
The coin you fling into his cap! And last,
Some bright morn, how men crowd about the midst
O' the market-place, where takes the old king breath
Ere with his crutch he strike the palace-gate
Wide ope!
To Turin, yes or no—or no?

[Re-enter **CHARLES** with papers.

CHARLES
Just as I thought! A miserable falsehood
Of hirelings discontented with their pay
And longing for enfranchisement! A few
Testy expressions of old age that thinks
To keep alive its dignity o'er slaves
By means that suit their natures!

[Tearing them.

Thus they shake
My faith in Victor!

[Turning, he discovers **VICTOR**.

VICTOR [After a pause]
Not at Evian, Charles?
What's this? Why do you run to close the doors?
No welcome for your father?

CHARLES [Aside]
Not his voice!

What would I give for one imperious tone
Of the old sort! That's gone forever.

VICTOR
Must
I ask once more ...

CHARLES
No—I concede it, sir!
You are returned for ... true, your health declines;
True, Chambery 's a bleak unkindly spot;
You 'd choose one fitter for your final lodge—
Veneria, or Moncaglier—ay, that's close
And I concede it.

VICTOR
I received advices
Of the conclusion of the Spanish matter,
Dated from Evian Baths ...

CHARLES
And you forbore
To visit me at Evian, satisfied
The work I had to do would fully task
The little wit I have, and that your presence
Would only disconcert me—

VICTOR
Charles?

CHARLES
—Me, set
Forever in a foreign course to yours,
And ...
Sir, this way of wile were good to catch,
But I have not the sleight of it. The truth!
Though I sink under it! What brings you here?

VICTOR
Not hope of this reception, certainly,
From one who 'd scarce assume a stranger mode
Of speech, did I return to bring about
Some awfullest calamity!

CHARLES
—You mean,
Did you require your crown again! Oh yes,
I should speak otherwise! But turn not that

To jesting! Sir, the truth! Your health declines?
Is aught deficient in your equipage?
Wisely you seek myself to make complaint,
And foil the malice of the world which laughs
At petty discontents; but I shall care
That not a soul knows of this visit. Speak!

VICTOR [Aside]
Here is the grateful much-professing son
Prepared to worship me, for whose sole sake
I think to waive my plans of public good!
[Aloud]
Nay, Charles, if I did seek to take once more
My crown, were so disposed to plague myself,
What would be warrant for this bitterness?
I gave it—grant I would resume it—well?

CHARLES
I should say simply—leaving out the why
And how—you made me swear to keep that crown:
And as you then intended ...

VICTOR
Fool! What way
Could I intend or not intend? As man,
With a man's will, when I say "I intend,"
I can intend up to a certain point,
No farther. I intended to preserve
The crown of Savoy and Sardinia whole:
And if events arise demonstrating
The way, I hoped should guard it, rather like
To lose it ...

CHARLES
Keep within your sphere and mine!
It is God's province we usurp on, else.
Here, blindfold through the maze of things we walk
By a slight clue of false, true, right and wrong;
All else is rambling and presumption. I
Have sworn to keep this kingdom: there's my truth.

VICTOR
Truth, boy, is here, within my breast; and in
Your recognition of it, truth is, too;
And in the effect of all this tortuous dealing
With falsehood, used to carry out the truth,
—In its success, this falsehood turns, again,
Truth for the world! But you are right: these themes

Are over-subtle. I should rather say
In such a case, frankly,—it fails, my scheme:
I hoped to see you bring about, yourself,
What I must bring about. I interpose
On your behalf—with my son's good in sight—
To hold what he is nearly letting go,
Confirm his title, add a grace perhaps.
There's Sicily, for instance,—granted me
And taken back, some years since: till I give
That island with the rest, my work's half done.
For his sake, therefore, as of those he rules ...

CHARLES

Our sakes are one; and that, you could not say,
Because my answer would present itself
Forthwith:—a year has wrought an age's change.
This people's not the people now, you once
Could benefit; nor is my policy
Your policy.

VICTOR [With an outburst]

I know it! You undo
All I have done—my life of toil and care!
I left you this the absolutest rule
In Europe: do you think I sit and smile,
Bid you throw power to the populace—
See my Sardinia, that has kept apart,
Join in the mad and democratic whirl
Whereto I see all Europe haste full tide?
England casts off her kings; France mimics England:
This realm I hoped was safe! Yet here I talk,
When I can save it, not by force alone,
But bidding plagues, which follow sons like you,
Fasten upon my disobedient ...

[Recollecting himself.

Surely
I could say this—if minded so—my son?

CHARLES

You could not. Bitterer curses than your curse
Have I long since denounced upon myself
If I misused my power. In fear of these
I entered on those measures—will abide
By them: so, I should say, Count Tende ...

VICTOR

No!
But no! But if, my Charles, your—more than old—
Half-foolish father urged these arguments,
And then confessed them futile, but said plainly
That he forgot his promise, found his strength
Fail him, had thought at savage Chambery
Too much of brilliant Turin, Rivoli here,
And Susa, and Veneria, and Superga—
Pined for the pleasant places he had built
When he was fortunate and young—

CHARLES
My father!

VICTOR
Stay yet!—and if he said he could not die
Deprived of baubles he had put aside,
He deemed, forever—of the Crown that binds
Your brain up, whole, sound and impregnable,
Creating kingliness—the Sceptre too,
Whose mere wind, should you wave it, back would beat
Invaders—and the golden Ball which throbs
As if you grasped the palpitating heart
Indeed o' the realm, to mould as choose you may!
—If I must totter up and down the streets
My sires built, where myself have introduced
And fostered laws and letters, sciences,
The civil and the military arts!
Stay, Charles! I see you letting me pretend
To live my former self once more—King Victor,
The venturous yet politic: they style me
Again, the Father of the Prince: friends wink
Good-humoredly at the delusion you
So sedulously guard from all rough truths
That else would break upon my dotage!—You—
Whom now I see preventing my old shame—
I tell not, point by cruel point, my tale—
For is't not in your breast my brow is hid?
Is not your hand extended? Say you not ...

[Enter **D'ORMEA**, leading in **POLYXENA**.

POLYXENA [Advancing and withdrawing **CHARLES**—to **VICTOR**]
In this conjuncture even, he would say
(Though with a moistened eye and quivering lip)
The suppliant is my father. I must save
A great man from himself, nor see him fling
His well-earned fame away: there must not follow

Ruin so utter, a break-down of worth
So absolute: no enemy shall learn,
He thrust his child 'twist danger and himself.
And, when that child somehow stood danger out,
Stole back with serpent wiles to ruin Charles
—Body, that's much,—and soul, that's more—and realm,
That's most of all! No enemy shall say ...

D'ORMEA
Do you repent, sir?

VICTOR [Resuming himself]
D'Ormea? This is well!
Worthily done, King Charles, craftily done!
Judiciously you post these, to o'erhear
The little your importunate father thrusts
Himself on you to say!—Ah, they'll correct
The amiable blind facility
You show in answering his peevish suit.
What can he need to sue for? Thanks, D'Ormea!
You have fulfilled your office: but for you,
The old Count might have drawn some few more livres
To swell his income! Had you, lady, missed
The moment, a permission might be granted
To buttress up my ruinous old pile!
But you remember properly the list
Of wise precautions I took when I gave
Nearly as much away—to reap the fruits
I should have looked for!

CHARLES
Thanks, sir: degrade me,
So you remain yourself! Adieu!

VICTOR
I'll not
Forget it for the future, nor presume
Next time to slight such mediators! Nay—
Had I first moved them both to intercede,
I might secure a chamber in Moncaglier
—Who knows?

CHARLES
Adieu!

VICTOR
You bid me this adieu
With the old spirit?

CHARLES
Adieu!

VICTOR
Charles—Charles!

CHARLES
Adieu!

[**VICTOR** goes.

CHARLES
You were mistaken, Marquis, as you hear!
'Twas for another purpose the Count came.
The Count desires Moncaglier. Give the order!

D'ORMEA [Leisurely]
Your minister has lost your confidence,
Asserting late, for his own purposes,
Count Tende would ...

CHARLES [Flinging his badge back]
Be still the minister!
And give a loose to your insulting joy;
It irks me more thus stifled than expressed:
Loose it!

D'ORMEA
There's none to loose, alas! I see
I never am to die a martyr.

POLYXENA
Charles!

CHARLES
No praise, at least, Polyxena—no praise!

KING CHARLES

PART II

D'ORMEA seated, folding papers he has been examining.

This at the last effects it: now, King Charles
Or else King Victor—that's a balance: but now,

D'Ormea the arch-culprit, either turn
Of the scale,—that's sure enough. A point to solve,
My masters, moralists, whate'er your style!
When you discover why I push myself
Into a pitfall you'd pass safely by,
Impart to me among the rest! No matter.
Prompt are the righteous ever with their rede
To us the wrongful: lesson them this once!
For safe among the wicked are you set,
D'Ormea! We lament life's brevity,
Yet quarter e'en the threescore years and ten,
Nor stick to call the quarter roundly "life."
D'Ormea was wicked, say, some twenty years;
A tree so long was stunted; afterward,
What if it grew, continued growing, till
No fellow of the forest equalled it?
'Twas a stump then; a stump it still must be:
While forward saplings, at the outset cheeked,
In virtue of that first sprout keep their style
Amid the forest's green fraternity.
Thus I shoot up to surely get lopped down
And bound up for the burning. Now for it!

[Enter **CHARLES** and **POLYXENA** with **ATTENDANTS**.

D'ORMEA [Rises]
Sir, in the due discharge of this my office—
This enforced summons of yourself from Turin,
And the disclosure I am bound to make
To-night,—there must already be, I feel,
So much that wounds ...

CHARLES
Well, sir?

D'ORMEA
—That I, perchance,
May utter also what, another time,
Would irk much,—it may prove less irksome now.

CHARLES
What would you utter?

D'ORMEA
That I from my soul
Grieve at to-night's event: for you I grieve,
E'en grieve for ...

CHARLES
Tush, another time for talk!
My kingdom is in imminent danger?

D'ORMEA
Let
The Count communicate with France—its King,
His grandson, will have Fleury's aid for this,
Though for no other war.

CHARLES
First for the levies:
What forces can I muster presently?

[**D'ORMEA** delivers papers which **CHARLES** inspects.

CHARLES
Good—very good. Montorio ... how is this?
—Equips me double the old complement
Of soldiers?

D'ORMEA
Since his land has been relieved
From double imposts, this he manages:
But under the late monarch ...

CHARLES
Peace! I know.
Count Spava has omitted mentioning
What proxy is to head these troops of his.

D'ORMEA
Count Spava means to head his troops himself.
Something to fight for now; "Whereas," says he,
"Under the sovereign's father" ...

CHARLES
It would seem
That all my people love me.

D'ORMEA
Yes.

[To **POLYXENA** while **CHARLES** continues to inspect the papers.

A temper
Like Victor's may avail to keep a state;
He terrifies men and they fall not off;

Good to restrain: best, if restraint were all.
But, with the silent circle round him, ends
Such sway: our King's begins precisely there.
For to suggest, impel and set at work,
Is quite another function. Men may slight,
In time of peace, the King who brought them peace:
In war,—his voice, his eyes, help more than fear.
They love you, sir!

CHARLES [To **ATTENDANTS**]
Bring the regalia, forth!
Quit the room! And now, Marquis, answer me!
Why should the King of France invade my realm?

D'ORMEA
Why? Did I not acquaint your Majesty
An hour ago?

CHARLES
I choose to hear again
What then I heard.

D'ORMEA
Because, sir, as I said,
Your father is resolved to have his crown
At any risk; and, as I judge, calls in
The foreigner to aid him.

CHARLES
And your reason
For saying this?

D'ORMEA [Aside]
Ay, just his father's way!
[To **CHARLES**]
The Count wrote yesterday to your forces' Chief,
Rhebinder—made demand of help—

CHARLES
To try
Rhebinder—he 's of alien blood. Aught else?

D'ORMEA
Receiving a refusal,—some hours after,
The Count called on Del Borgo to deliver
The Act of Abdication: he refusing,
Or hesitating, rather—

CHARLES
What ensued?

D'ORMEA
At midnight, only two hours since, at Turin,
He rode in person to the citadel
With one attendant, to Soccorso gate,
And bade the governor, San Remi, open—
Admit him.

CHARLES
For a purpose I divine.
These three were faithful, then?

D'ORMEA
They told it me:
And I—

CHARLES
Most faithful—

D'ORMEA
Tell it you—with this
Moreover of my own: if, an hour hence,
You have not interposed, the Count will be
O' the road to France for succor.

CHARLES
Very good!
You do your duty now to me your monarch
Fully, I warrant?—have, that is, your project
For saving both of us disgrace, no doubt?

D'ORMEA
I give my counsel,—and the only one.
A month since, I besought you to employ
Restraints which had prevented many a pang:
But now the harsher course must be pursued.
These papers, made for the emergency,
Will pain you to subscribe: this is a list
Of those suspected merely—men to watch;
This—of the few of the Count's very household
You must, however reluctantly, arrest;
While here's a method of remonstrance—sure
Not stronger than the case demands—to take
With the Count's self.

CHARLES

Deliver those three papers.

POLYXENA [While **CHARLES** inspects them—to **D'ORMEA**]
Your measures are not over-harsh, sir: France
Will hardly be deterred from her intents
By these.

D'ORMEA
If who proposes might dispose,
I could soon satisfy you. Even these,
Hear what he'll say at my presenting!

CHARLES [who has signed them]
There!
About the warrants! You've my signature.
What turns you pale? I do my duty by you
In acting boldly thus on your advice.

D'ORMEA [Reading them separately]
Arrest the people I
suspected merely?

CHARLES
Did you suspect them?

D'ORMEA
Doubtless: but—but—sir,
This Forquieri's governor of Turin,
And Rivarol and he have influence over
Half of the capital! Rabella, too?
Why, sir—

CHARLES
Oh, leave the fear to me!

D'ORMEA [Still reading]
You bid me
Incarcerate the people on this list?
Sir—

CHARLES
But you never bade arrest those men,
So close related to my father too,
On trifling grounds?

D'ORMEA
Oh, as for that, St. George,
President of Chambery's senators,

Is hatching treason! still—
[More troubled]
Sir, Count Cumiane
Is brother to your father's wife! What 's here?
Arrest the wife herself?

CHARLES
You seem to think
A venial crime this plot against me. Well?

D'ORMEA [who has read the last paper]
Wherefore am I thus ruined?
Why not take
My life at once? This poor formality
Is, let me say, unworthy you! Prevent it
You, madam! I have served you, am prepared
For all disgraces: only, let disgrace
Be plain, be proper—proper for the world
To pass its judgment on 'twixt you and me!
Take back your warrant, I will none of it!

CHARLES
Here is a man to talk of fickleness!
He stakes his life upon my father's falsehood;
I bid him ...

D'ORMEA
Not you! Were he trebly false,
You do not bid me ...

CHARLES
Is 't not written there?
I thought so: give—I 'll set it right.

D'ORMEA
Is it there?
Oh yes, and plain—arrest him now—drag here
Your father! And were all six times as plain,
Do you suppose I trust it?

CHARLES
Just one word!
You bring him, taken in the act of flight,
Or else your life is forfeit.

D'ORMEA
Ay, to Turin
I bring him, and to-morrow?

CHARLES
Here and now!
The whole thing is a lie, a hateful lie,
As I believed and as my father said.
I knew it from the first, but was compelled
To circumvent you; and the great D'Ormea,
That baffled Alberoni and tricked Coscia,
The miserable sower of such discord
'Twixt sire and son, is in the toils at last.
Oh I see! you arrive—this plan of yours,
Weak as it is, torments sufficiently
A sick old peevish man—wrings hasty speech,
An ill-considered threat from him; that's noted;
Then out you ferret papers, his amusement
In lonely hours of lassitude—examine
The day-by-day report of your paid spies—
And back you come: all was not ripe, you find,
And, as you hope, may keep from ripening yet,
But you were in bare time! Only, 'twere best
I never saw my father—these old men
Are potent in excuses: and meanwhile,
D'Ormea's the man I cannot do without!

POLYXENA
Charles—

CHARLES
Ah, no question! You against me too!
You 'd have me eat and drink and sleep, live, die,
With this lie coiled about me, choking me!
No, no, D'Ormea! You venture life, you say,
Upon my father's perfidy: and I
Have, on the whole, no right to disregard
The chains of testimony you thus wind
About me; though I do—do from my soul
Discredit them: still I must authorize
These measures, and I will. Perugia!

[Many **OFFICERS** enter.

Count—
You and Solar, with all the force you have,
Stand at the Marquis' orders: what he bids,
Implicitly perform! You are to bring
A traitor here; the man that 's likest one
At present, fronts me; you are at his beck
For a full hour! he undertakes to show

A fouler than himself,—but, failing that,
Return with him, and, as my father lives,
He dies this night! The clemency you blame
So oft, shall be revoked—rights exercised,
Too long abjured.
[To **D'ORMEA**]
Now, sir, about the work!
To save your king and country! Take the warrant!

D'ORMEA
You hear the sovereign's mandate, Count Perugia?
Obey me! As your diligence, expect
Reward! All follow to Montcaglier!

[**D'ORMEA** goes.

CHARLES [In great anguish]
D'Ormea!
He goes, lit up with that appalling smile!

[To **POLYXENA** after a pause.

At least you understand all this?

POLYXENA
These means
Of our defence—these measures of precaution?

CHARLES
It must be the best way: I should have else
Withered beneath his scorn.

POLYXENA
What would you say?

CHARLES
Why, do you think I mean to keep the crown, Polyxena?

POLYXENA
You then believe the story
In spite of all—that Victor comes?

CHARLES
Believe it?
I know that he is coming—feel the strength
That has upheld me leave me at his coming!
'T was mine, and now he takes his own again.
Some kinds of strength are well enough to have;

But who 's to have that strength? Let my crown go!
I meant to keep it; but I cannot—cannot!
Only, he shall not taunt me—he, the first ...
See if he would not be the first to taunt me
With having left his kingdom at a word,
With letting it be conquered without stroke,
With ... no—no—'t is no worse than when he left!
I 've just to bid him take it, and, that over,
We 'll fly away—fly, for I loathe this Turin,
This Rivoli, all titles loathe, all state.
We 'd best go to your country—unless God
Send I die now!

POLYXENA
Charles, hear me!

CHARLES
And again
Shall you be my Polyxena—you 'll take me
Out of this woe! Yes, do speak, and keep speaking!
I would not let you speak just now, for fear
You 'd counsel me against him: but talk, now,
As we two used to talk in blessed times:
Bid me endure all his caprices; take me
From this mad post above him!

POLYXENA
I believe
We are undone, but from a different cause.
All your resources, down to the least guard,
Are at D'Ormea's beck. What if, the while,
He act in concert with your father? We
Indeed were lost. This lonely Rivoli—
Where find a better place for them?

CHARLES [Pacing the room]
And why
Does Victor come? To undo all that 's done,
Restore the past, prevent the future! Seat
His mistress in your seat, and place in mine
... Oh, my own people, whom will you find there,
To ask of, to consult with, to care for,
To hold up with your hands? Whom? One that's false—
False—from the head's crown to the foot's sole, false!
The best is, that I knew it in my heart
From the beginning, and expected this,
And hated you, Polyxena, because
You saw through him, though I too saw through him,

Saw that he meant this while he crowned me, while
He prayed for me,—nay, while he kissed my brow,
I saw—

POLYXENA
But if your measures take effect,
D'Ormea true to you?

CHARLES
Then worst of all!
I shall have loosed that callous wretch on him!
Well may the woman taunt him with his child—
I, eating here his bread, clothed in his clothes,
Seated upon his seat, let slip D'Ormea
To outrage him! We talk—perchance he tears
My father from his bed; the old hands feel
For one who is not, but who should be there:
He finds D'Ormea! D'Ormea too finds him!
The crowded chamber when the lights go out—
Closed doors—the horrid scuffle in the dark—
The accursed prompting of the minute! My guards!
To horse—and after, with me—and prevent!

POLYXENA [Seizing his hand]
King Charles! Pause here upon this strip of time
Allotted you out of eternity!
Crowns are from God: you in his name hold yours.
Your life 's no least thing, were it your life
Should be abjured along with rule; but now,
Keep both! Your duty is to live and rule—
You, who would vulgarly look fine enough
In the world's eye, deserting your soul's charge,—
Ay, you would have men's praise, this Rivoli
Would be illumined! While, as 't is, no doubt,
Something of stain will ever rest on you;
No one will rightly know why you refused
To abdicate; they 'll talk of deeds you could
Have done, no doubt,—nor do I much expect
Future achievement will blot out the past,
Envelope it in haze—nor shall we two
Live happy any more. 'T will be, I feel,
Only in moments that the duty 's seen
As palpably as now: the months, the years
Of painful indistinctness are to come,
While daily must we tread these palace-rooms
Pregnant with memories of the past: your eye
May turn to mine and find no comfort there,
Through fancies that beset me, as yourself,

Of other courses, with far other issues,
We might have taken this great night: such bear,
As I will bear! What matters happiness?
Duty! There's man's one moment: this is yours!

[Putting the crown on his head, and the sceptre in his hand, she places him on his seat: a long pause and silence.

[Enter **D'ORMEA** and **VICTOR**, with **GUARDS**.

VICTOR
At last I speak; but once—that once, to you!
'T is you I ask, not these your varletry,
Who 's King of us?

CHARLES [From his seat]
Count Tende ...

VICTOR
What your spies
Assert I ponder in my soul, I say—
Here to your face, amid your guards! I choose
To take again the crown whose shadow I gave—
For still its potency surrounds the weak
White locks their felon hands have discomposed.
Or I 'll not ask who 's King, but simply, who
Withholds the crown I claim? Deliver it!
I have no friend in the wide world: nor France
Nor England cares for me: you see the sum
Of what I can avail. Deliver it!

CHARLES
Take it, my father!
And now say in turn,
Was it done well, my father—sure not well,
To try me thus! I might have seen much cause
For keeping it—too easily seen cause!
But, from that moment, e'en more woefully
My life had pined away, than pine it will.
Already you have much to answer for.
My life to pine is nothing,—her sunk eyes
Were happy once! No doubt, my people think
I am their King still ... but I cannot strive!
Take it!

VICTOR [One hand on the crown **CHARLES** offers, the other on his neck]
So few years give it quietly,
My son! It will drop from me. See you not?

A crown 's unlike a sword to give away—
That, let a strong hand to a weak hand give!
But crowns should slip from palsied brows to heads
Young as this head: yet mine is weak enough,
E'en weaker than I knew. I seek for phrases
To vindicate my right. 'T is of a piece!
All is alike gone by with me—who beat
Once D'Orleans in his lines—his very lines!
To have been Eugene's comrade, Louis's rival,
And now ...

CHARLES [Putting the crown on him, to the rest]
The King speaks, yet none kneels, I think!

VICTOR
I am then King! As I became a King
Despite the nations, kept myself a King,
So I die King, with Kingship dying too
Around me! I have lasted Europe's time!
What wants my story of completion? Where
Must needs the damning break show? Who mistrusts
My children here—tell they of any break
'Twixt my day's sunrise and its fiery fall?
And who were by me when I died but they?
D'Ormea there!

CHARLES
What means he?

VICTOR
Ever there!
Charles—how to save your story! Mine must go!
Say—say that you refused the crown to me!
Charles, yours shall be my story! You immured
Me, say, at Rivoli. A single year
I spend without a sight of you, then die.
That will serve every purpose—tell that tale
The world!

CHARLES
Mistrust me? Help!

VICTOR
Past help, past reach!
'T is in the heart—you cannot reach the heart:
This broke mine, that I did believe, you, Charles,
Would have denied me and disgraced me.

POLYXENA
Charles
Has never ceased to be your subject, sir!
He reigned at first through setting up yourself
As pattern: if he e'er seemed harsh to you,
'T was from a too intense appreciation
Of your own character: he acted you—
Ne'er for an instant did I think it real,
Nor look for any other than this end.
I hold him worlds the worse on that account;
But so it was.

CHARLES [To **POLYXENA**]
I love you now indeed!
[To **VICTOR**]
You never knew me!

VICTOR
Hardly till this moment,
When I seem learning many other things
Because the time for using them is past.
If 't were to do again! That's idly wished.
Truthfulness might prove policy as good
As guile. Is this my daughter's forehead? Yes:
I 've made it fitter now to be a queen's
Than formerly: I 've ploughed the deep lines there
Which keep too well a crown from slipping off.
No matter. Guile has made me King again.
Louis—'t was in King Victor's time:—long since,
When Louis reigned and, also, Victor reigned.
How the world talks already of us two!
God of eclipse and each discolored star,
Why do I linger then?
Ha! Where lurks he?
D'Ormea! Nearer to your King! Now stand!

[Collecting his strength as **D'ORMEA** approaches.

You lied, D'Ormea! I do not repent.

[Dies.

He is the equal of any Victorian Poet that could be mentioned. However, Browning continues to be in the shadow of Tennyson, Arnold, Hopkins, Morris and many others.

Robert Browning was born on May 7th, 1812 in Walworth in the parish of Camberwell, London. He was baptized on June 14th, 1812, at Lock's Fields Independent Chapel, York Street, Walworth.

Browning's early years were certainly very interesting. His mother was an excellent pianist and a very devout evangelical Christian. His father, who worked as a clerk at the Bank of England, was also an artist, scholar, antiquarian, and collector of books and pictures. Indeed, he amassed more than 6,000 volumes of rare books including works in Greek, Hebrew, Latin, French, Italian, and Spanish. For the young and curious Browning, it was a wonderful resource, added to which his father was a guiding force in his education.

Many accounts attest that Browning was already proficient at reading and writing by the age of five. He is said to have been a bright but anxious student and to have studied and learnt Latin, Greek, and French by the time he was fourteen. From fourteen to sixteen he was educated at home, tutored in music, drawing, dancing, and horsemanship. Certainly, language and the arts were two areas the young Browning both absorbed and pushed himself towards.

At the age of twelve he wrote a volume of Byronic verse he called Incondita, which his parents attempted to have published. The attempts were unsuccessful and, disappointed, Browning destroyed the work.

In 1825, a cousin gave Browning a collection of Percy Bysshe Shelley's poetry; Browning was so enamored with the poems that he asked for the rest of Shelley's works for his thirteenth birthday. In fact, Browning then went the extra mile, declaring himself to be both a vegetarian and an atheist in honour of his hero.

Intriguingly it seems that the rejection of his first volume didn't dim his appreciation of other poets, but it appears to have stopped him writing any poems between the ages of thirteen and twenty.

In 1828, Browning enrolled at the newly-opened University of London. He was uncomfortable with the experience and he soon left, anxious to read and absorb at his own pace.

His education which, overall is notably rambling and lacks a structure that many of his artistic contemporaries enjoyed, i.e. excellent public schooling and then a degree at Oxford or Cambridge, may present many of his critics with ammunition to criticize, but alternatively his hap-hazard education certainly contributed to many of the references that baffled both critics and his audience, but they tellingly show the breath and scale of what he could turn words too. What others would call obscure references were, to Browning, remarkably obvious.

Browning's early career was very promising. His long poem Pauline (of which only a fragment was ever finished and published) brought him to the attention of the Pre-Raphaelite master Dante Gabriel Rossetti and his difficult Paracelsus (published in 1835) was warmly admired by both Dickens and Wordsworth.

In the 1830s he met the actor William Macready and was encouraged to develop and turn his talents to the stage by writing verse drama. But these plays, including Strafford, which ran for five nights in 1837, and those contained within the Bells and Pomegranates series, were, for the most part, unsuccessful.

During this period Browning began to discover that his real talents lay in taking a single character and allowing that character to discover more about himself by revealing further personal aspects of himself in his speeches; the dramatic monologue. The techniques he developed through this—especially the use of diction, rhythm, and symbol—are regarded as his most important contribution to poetry. They would later influence such major poets of the 20th Century as Ezra Pound, T. S. Eliot, and Robert Frost.

By 1840, with the publication of Sordello, the tide turned somewhat. Many thought he was being deliberately obscure, opaque beyond measure and his poetry for the next decade or so was not eagerly acquired or talked about.

As Browning attempted to rehabilitate his career he began a relationship with Elizabeth Barrett in 1845. He had read her poems and, being totally charmed by their quality, was determined to meet her. The poetess was better known than the younger Browning but suffered from a debilitating illness and was also subject to the harsh behaviour of her over-bearing father. Nevertheless, the new couple were soon inseparable.

Her father, as he did with any of his children that married, disinherited her. Despite this she had some money from her own resources and sensing that the best outcome for both the relationship and her own health was to move abroad the couple did just that. After a private marriage at St Marylebone Parish Church, in September 1846, they journeyed to Europe to honeymoon in Paris.

Their new life now took them to Italy, first to Pisa and a little later to Florence. There they absorbed life and one another.

But in the short term the literary assault on Browning's work did not let up. He was now criticized by such patrician writers as Charles Kingsley for his abandonment of England for foreign lands. Browning could do little to answer these attacks except to compose with his pen and continue with his poetical journey.

The Browning's were well respected, and even famous. Elizabeth health began to improve, she grew stronger and in 1849, at the age of 43, between four miscarriages, she gave birth to a son, Robert Wiedeman Barrett Browning, whom they nicknamed "Penini" or "Pen",

Intriguingly despite his growing reputation and return to form as a poet he was more often than not known as 'Elizabeth Barrett's husband'.

Work flowed from his pen that was to ensure his reputation as one of England's leading poets. When his collection Men and Women was published in 1855 it contained some of his finest lines. It was dedicated to Elizabeth. Life had begun to smile handsome rewards upon the Brownings.

Victorian society was very much taken with all things spiritualist. It was not enough to have command of much of the globe through Empire, they wished to know and explore wherever they could. The spirit world beckoned their interest. Browning dissented from this view believing it was all a hoax and a fraud. Elizabeth, however, was inclined to believe and this caused several disagreements between the couple.

They attended a séance by Daniel Dunglas Home, in July 1855. (Home was a famous and clamored after Scottish physical medium with the reported ability to levitate and speak with the dead). It is said that during this séance a spirit face materialised. Home then claimed it was the face of Browning's son who had died in infancy. Browning seized the 'materialisation' which turned out to be Home's bare foot. Browning had never lost a son in infancy.

After the séance, Browning wrote an angry letter to The Times, in which he said: "the whole display of hands, spirit utterances etc., was a cheat and imposture."

The Browning's time in Italy were immensely rewarding years for both their personal and professional lives. Browning encouraged her to include Sonnets from the Portuguese in her published works, these beautiful poems are undoubtedly one of the highlights of English love poetry.

Elizabeth had become quite politicised during these years. Engrossed in Italian politics (which was continuing to slowly re-unify the country), she issued a small volume of political poems entitled Poems before Congress (1860) most of which were written to express her sympathy with the Italian cause after the earlier outbreak of The Second Italian Independence War in 1859. In England they caused uproar. Conservative magazines such as Blackwood's and the Saturday Review labelled her a fanatic. She dedicated the book to her husband.

But in 1861 tragedy struck.

The couple had spent the winter of 1860–61 in Rome when Elizabeth's health deteriorated again and they returned to Florence in early June. However, these turned out to be her final weeks. Only morphine would now still the pain. She died in Browning's arms on June 29th, 1861. Browning said that she died "smilingly, happily, and with a face like a girl's .... Her last word was .... "Beautiful".

Her burial took place in the nearby Protestant English Cemetery of Florence. The local people were deeply saddened, and shops closed their doors in grief and respect.

Browning and their son were obviously devastated. Unable to bear being in Florence without Elizabeth they soon returned to London to live at 19 Warwick Crescent, Maida Vale.

As he re-integrated himself back into the London literary scene he began to finally receive the proper praise, respect and reputation that his works deserved.

Browning went on to publish Dramatis Personæ (1864), and The Ring and the Book (1868–1869). The latter, based on an "old yellow book" which told of a seventeenth-century Italian murder trial, received wide and generous critical acclaim. Although by now he was in the twilight of a long and prolific career, that had achieved some notable ups and downs, he was respected and indeed renowned for his talents and works.

In 1878, he revisited Italy for the first time since Elizabeth's death. He would return there on several further occasions but never to Florence.

Such was the esteem he was held in that The Browning Society was founded in 1881. Although he had never obtained a degree (something that set him apart from many other Victorian poets) he was now awarded honorary degrees from Oxford University in 1882 and then the University of Edinburgh in 1884.

In 1887, Browning produced the major work of his later years, Parleyings with Certain People of Importance in Their Day. Browning now spoke with his own voice as he engaged in a series of dialogues with long-forgotten figures of literary, artistic, and philosophic history. Unfortunately, both the critics and public were completely baffled by this.

On April 7th, 1889 Browning attended a dinner party at the home of his friend, the artist Rudolf Lehmann. The highlight of which was a recording made on a wax cylinder on an Edison cylinder phonograph. On the recording, which still exists, Browning recites part of How They Brought the Good News from Ghent to Aix, and can even be heard apologising when he forgets the words.

The recording was first played in 1890 on the anniversary of his death, at a gathering of his admirers, it was said to be the first time anyone's voice 'had been heard from beyond the grave'.

His last work Asolando: Fancies and Facts (1889), returned to his brief and concise lyric verse that was so popular. It was published on the day of his death on December 12th, 1889, Robert Browning was at his son's home Ca' Rezzonico in Venice.

He was buried in Poets' Corner in Westminster Abbey; his grave lies immediately adjacent to that of Alfred Tennyson.

Among the many who have publicly acknowledged their literary debt to him are Henry James, Oscar Wilde, George Bernard Shaw, G. K. Chesterton, Ezra Pound, Jorge Luis Borges, and Vladimir Nabokov.

Robert Browning - A Concise Bibliography

Here follows a list of the plays and poetry volumes published during his lifetime. Poems of particular worth are noted from within those volumes.

Pauline: A Fragment of a Confession (1833)
Paracelsus (1835)
Strafford (play) (1837)
Sordello (1840)
Bells and Pomegranates No. I: Pippa Passes (play) (1841)
    The Year's at the Spring
Bells and Pomegranates No. II: King Victor and King Charles (play) (1842)
Bells and Pomegranates No. III: Dramatic Lyrics (1842)
    Porphyria's Lover
    Soliloquy of the Spanish Cloister
    My Last Duchess
    The Pied Piper of Hamelin
    Count Gismond
    Johannes Agricola in Meditation

Bells and Pomegranates No. IV: The Return of the Druses (play) (1843)
Bells and Pomegranates No. V: A Blot in the 'Scutcheon (play) (1843)
Bells and Pomegranates No. VI: Colombe's Birthday (play) (1844)
Bells and Pomegranates No. VII: Dramatic Romances and Lyrics (1845)

> *The Laboratory*
> *How They Brought the Good News from Ghent to Aix*
> *The Bishop Orders His Tomb at Saint Praxed's Church*
> *The Lost Leader*
> *Home Thoughts from Abroad*
> *Meeting at Night*

Bells and Pomegranates No. VIII: Luria and A Soul's Tragedy (plays) (1846)
Christmas-Eve and Easter-Day (1850)
An Essay on Percy Bysshe Shelley (essay) (1852)
Two Poems (1854)
Men and Women (1855)

> *Love Among the Ruins*
> *A Toccata of Galuppi's*
> *Childe Roland to the Dark Tower Came*
> *Fra Lippo Lippi*
> *Andrea Del Sarto*
> *The Patriot*
> *The Last Ride Together*
> *Memorabilia*
> *Cleon*
> *How It Strikes a Contemporary*
> *The Statue and the Bust*
> *A Grammarian's Funeral*
> *An Epistle Containing the Strange Medical Experience of Karshish, the Arab Physician*
> *Bishop Blougram's Apology*
> *Master Hugues of Saxe-Gotha*
> *By the Fire-side*

Dramatis Personae (1864)

> *Caliban upon Setebos*
> *Rabbi Ben Ezra*
> *Abt Vogler*
> *Mr. Sludge, "The Medium"*
> *Prospice*
> *A Death in the Desert*

The Ring and the Book (1868–69)
Balaustion's Adventure (1871)
Prince Hohenstiel-Schwangau, Saviour of Society (1871)
Fifine at the Fair (1872)
Red Cotton Night-Cap Country, or, Turf and Towers (1873)
Aristophanes' Apology (1875)

> *Thamuris Marching*

The Inn Album (1875)
Pacchiarotto, and How He Worked in Distemper (1876)

> *Numpholeptos*

The Agamemnon of Aeschylus (1877)
La Saisiaz and The Two Poets of Croisic (1878)
Dramatic Idylls (1879)
Dramatic Idylls: Second Series (1880)
    Pan and Luna
Jocoseria (1883)
Ferishtah's Fancies (1884)
Parleyings with Certain People of Importance in Their Day (1887)
Asolando (1889)
    Prologue
    Summum Bonum
    Bad Dreams III
    Flute-Music, with an Accompaniment
    Epilogue

www.ingramcontent.com/pod-product-compliance
Lightning Source LLC
Chambersburg PA
CBHW060049050426
42448CB00011B/2360